# No Other Kind
## of World

Also by Jeff Hardin

*Small Revolution*
*Restoring the Narrative*
*Notes for a Praise Book*
*Fall Sanctuary*

# No Other Kind of World

Jeff Hardin

Texas Review Press
Huntsville, Texas

FIRST EDITION

Requests for permission to acknowledge material from the work should be sent to:

**Permissions**
Texas Review Press
English Department
Sam Houston State University
Huntsville, TX 77341-2146

**Cover art** by Fred Behrens
**Author photo** by Eli Hardin
**Cover design** by Nancy Parsons, www.graphicdesigngroup.net

**Library of Congress Cataloging-in-Publication Data**

Names: Hardin, Jeff, 1968- author.

Title: No other kind of world / by Jeff Hardin.

Description: First edition. | Huntsville, Texas : Texas Review Press, [2017]

Identifiers: LCCN 2017026582 (print) | LCCN 2017030304 (ebook) | ISBN
9781680031362 | ISBN 9781680031355 (pbk.)

Subjects: | LCGFT: Poetry. | Ghazals (Poetry)

Classification: LCC PS3558.A623 (ebook) | LCC PS3558.A623 A6 2017 (print) |
DDC 811/.54--dc23

LC record available at https://lccn.loc.gov/2017026582

*celebrating my grandparents, Gip and Frances Hardin
and my father, Jimmy Hardin*

# Contents:

# No Other Kind
# of World

# IMMEASURABLE

Having read and loved a poem by Neruda,
    good luck finding it again
in all those pages, book after book.

And a passage, stanza, or phrase?
    Might as well reach inside a waterfall,
pull out a lily or lighthouse—

the words will have turned already
    to enigma or shade of acacia trees,
an incoming wave on the sand.

And forget trying to place again a single word,
    the one from which you felt a shiver.
It has pledged itself to silence, wind,

aroma of some yesterday only your bones can know.
    You are now a servant of uncertainties.
Having known and moved among borders;

having sailed through open doors and solitudes
    and danced upon pollen, your mouth
open, tasting a pulse on the air;

having touched surf and shawl and the rain
    inside piano notes lingering all night,
now you know nothing, a child again

who picks up rocks, tosses them into a stream,
    each disappearing for perhaps millennia
or never to be touched again, like a thought.

# A DIFFERENT COUNTRY

It's clear now we'd have a different
country had Ed Sullivan featured
poets—I mean, you can watch
only so many drummers twirling
drumsticks before you just have
to shrug and go back to stirring
penne pasta.
                     For all the talk
of the British Invasion, it never did
what Bly's poems were doing, sending
us out into silences, onto roads
deserted all night.
                     Or Neruda—
writing to sadness, needing its
black wing, his own blood
to go slow, slow, yeah, yeah,
for he wanted to receive inside him
the rain's trembling hands.
                              Imagine
Stafford's quiet voice as households
gathered for the evening's really
big show in dear detail, by ideal
light, the whole country occupied,
small towns of sirens where nothing
was solved.
                     Yes, in the name of
love, we should have stopped
to hear Bishop's marvelous stove,
grandmother and child with almanac
and tears in a house much like
our own.
                     Wendell Berry was just
breaking ground and Heaney fingering
mud slime, savoring dropped buckets
down wells still echoing.

                    Please,
Mr. Postman, send us a different
letter than the ones we've always
opened, maybe the ones Dickinson
said she wrote with pens unseen;
though she had no forum or supporters,
she loves us, we're loved, she said so,
and you know
                    that can't be bad.

# HOW MANY LIVES DO YOU HAVE?

*a response to Eli's question*

Aesop cannot find a moral to my life, while
Basho tucks me in his knapsack, strikes out on a journey.
Camus turns down the café lights and occupies himself.
Dostoyevsky whispers in my ear and, running, I can't hide.
Emerson, at my funeral, shows up to read my journals' genius thoughts.
Frost leaves me in the snow-filled woods then hides his path's escape.
Goethe blows upon the pile of ashes I've become to breed a fire.
Hopkins harrow-haunts my hopes, arrests my daily wrestlings.
Issa mourns the loss of time that holds us both within its care, though
Jeffers gives the world back to itself without my selfish taint.
Kabir's ecstatic that I've walked out back to toss the scraps that
Li Po scrambles from the woods to sniff and steal away.
Melville bellows, throws doubloons about my feet, to which
Neruda writes some skinny odes that reek of mist and sea wrack.
O'Connor plays a chess game with my soul, her story's only character.
Proust knows I love the wind to last for days across the window screen.
Quasimodo takes his half of a parabola while I tremble holding mine.
Rilke sends me stacks and stacks of letters, rose petals tucked inside.
Stafford knows my face and name, says give them both away.
Transtromer shadows me, sneaks up behind, whispers, "Guess who?"
Ungaretti sings the music of a single word until the singing, too, is sung.
Vallejo walks across the street to place a crumb inside my mouth.
Whitman nods to me, the two of us hid out beneath the silence of the stars.
Xenophanes says together we'll revise those other poets' blasphemies.
Yeats gets down a book whose fragrant pages drift inside my dreams.
Zagajewski convinces me that I'm Linnaeus and everything's misnamed.

# PLENITUDE

Sit in the sun.
        Out under the sky

and beside the same field
        as always,

which is not as before
        or as will be

but is and is.
        To scan around:

a plenitude of unfolding,
        of the suddenly there

to inhabit,
        take up residence in,

look through, look out from,
        hide within and find breath,

be translated unto
        or out of.

A brushstroke of feathers:
        interruption

against the clouds
        interrupting the blue

—I may be,
        against the landscapes,

just as there
        then gone,

a spokenness heard
        then barely remembered,

a rift in time
        sealing back up.

Do I consent to,
        give assent to,

stand in the radiant,
        slender whisper

of the name I am?
        He maketh me

to lie down,
        but I get back up,

kick the leaves along,
        try to touch

that yellowing shade
        at the far reach of sky

or held at the tip edge
        of grass blades.

Told, years ago,
        we are vessels,

I still believe the words,
        the words themselves

holding forth
        my faith placed in them.

I would whisper them all,
        say them

so that even I
>would need to listen

as an intimate,
>as the bloom does

to the bee,
>as a leaf does

to the ripple
>it touches forth

from a pond,
>as one word

must hear a next word,
>a next word.

And the sound of them
>making a shape

of their movement.
>And this shape

leading my mouth
>to what's knowable.

What's knowable
>trembling

to be so near
>to what's not.

Existence:  here,
>in the place of here,

in the here of now,
>in the now

of no longer here.
            Echo of an echo.

For what
            am I a vessel?

What shall I contain
            if not the space

across which
            such an echo moves

to find a shape,
            a reach?

A flowing
            as wind flows

when grass leans
            to let it.

A day large enough
            to hold

an evening field.
            What a field holds.

# IN WINTER

the pine trees' limbs
        fill with snow,
grow tense

with being on the verge—
        if not from weight,
then from suspense—

of crashing down
        along this length
of side-yard fence,

which, admittedly,
        is little more
than pretense

and holds nothing in
        but nonetheless
provides a lens,

a frame, through which
        most evenings I admire
a late-light rinse

down the barn's roof
        of fifty years
of hedge-apple dents,

there where, a child,
        I often climbed
but haven't since,

though where else, where else
        ever felt so soul-small
and immense.

# PROSOPAGNOSIA

I know, in America, we think ourselves David
holding a stone,
                    ready to leap toward the fight,
but what if it turns out, instead, we're the giant.

Too few people have decided to fail, to step
to the side so another can stretch toward the finish line.
From the swallows we learn
                    how to swap who will lead.

You and I have spent centuries telling our stories,
one to another, face to face, in this smallest of rooms.
Even Frost, in his sestets,
                    didn't reach clear conclusions.

I want the original version, Magritte's Still Life
or those pair of initials, hidden by Leonardo
in Mona Lisa's eyes,
                    he thought would never be found.

In you, in me, one has to wonder what God
has hidden
            —a weeping for piano notes entwined
or for the moment the goose far behind catches up.

# ALWAYS UPSTREAM OR DOWNSTREAM

We'd push out in an old canoe to float Horse creek,
fishing poles in hand, a Maxwell House can of red worms
dug up from a place we kept a secret past the barn.
Maybe we had all day—who knows—and maybe a day
meant nothing to us, for all of eternity belonged
to the wind on our faces and the slip-slap sound
of the paddle seeking cool and dark-green, still pools
thick with bream and bass and slick-bellied catfish.
Someone had told us catfish were mythic creatures
that could rise up to walk on water and up the slick banks
to perch themselves in cottonwoods; and maybe they could,
but we never saw them, always upstream or downstream
and never quite lonely enough in our hearts. Albert,
who was not my brother by blood but whose memory
on earth I'll fight you for, would take his rod and reel,
bait the hook with such a gentleness, a patience—
he made a music of it, a visionary music
in praise of fish hid out beneath decaying logs
or sunning themselves in shallows. Such iridescence,
olive and yellow—such craft of dorsal fin and gills.
And the two of us stalled in the middle of nowhere,
the only two people in the history of the world
who would ever see these fish! His cast was flawless,
smooth, almost silent, a balletic motion despite the limbs
we had to navigate. The world believed its wars
and greed, believed its clocks and fame and arguments
of history, while silence seemed to push at us
from every side, until the boat bumped the creek bed.
Even now the bliss of that surprise, the memory of it,
the climbing out to drag and tug, to hear the grit
of an existence that sometimes must be hauled
from one dry place to deeper water. Men grow old
to learn a young boy's trust of everything that is;

but Albert won't grow old, just young and younger,
forever tying flies, biting off the excess string,
trailing his hand in the coolest water of earth;
and I'll grow old and older, the wide world filling up
with loss of all we ever saw and marveled at
there on that creek from which long summers go on drinking.

# COUNTY HOME ROAD

Remember the smell of chicken coops,
that hideous labor of squawking
that rose to fever-pitched crescendos
each time you stepped inside the door.
They knew you for the thief you were
under the guise of acting curious.
And back of the barn you aimed slim rocks
to stun the sunlight sheet-metal flung.
Later, a trail. Through the woods it only
circled back upon itself and left you
nowhere new. You were seven or eight,
one more life somehow dropped down
amid tractors and unplowed fields,
a pig pen of mud and corn shucks,
and just around the bend of the road
a stretch of honeysuckle obscuring fence rows.
Those long nights waiting for a mother
who never came home, drunk in a bar—
you'd lift the window just a little,
see the moon afloat and the oak limbs
stretch to catch it, see the reach of sky
that reached nothing you wanted anyway.
You'd slip a thin wrist beneath and out
and into the windy night, feel that cool
air blowing in from distant lands,
across deserts and mountains and along
this fencerow, to brush across your hand.
Let's not summon forth pity or tenderness
or any other myth that makes the moment
more than what it was. Let's not judge,
mourn, or shame ourselves with wondering how
this boy will ever make it, how he won't
for all his life, as others sleep, lie in the sweat

of his body, listening to owl calls across
the pasture and footfalls from the edge
of the woods.  He was just a boy
who couldn't sleep.  He raised the window
for air, as anyone would, and clutched
a tight fist of nothingness, as anyone would;
and when he woke, the hand was there,
like an offering, and filled with morning dew.

# ON THE EVE OF A NEW MILLENNIUM

Drunk off his can and pissed at the ruse of another day,
back-ache a bum rap and woodpile shrunk to kindling,
the old man stood at the kitchen sink and stared out
at his neighbor's cow. What a filthy beast, he thought.
What a stinking, cud-chewing, gas-spewing waste of a field.
And then, because what else should happen on a day as dull
as this one, what better way to stun the silence out of all
it cannot say, he stumbled through the ashen rooms to find
his gun. The front room table spilled its stack of magazines
and pens. He was not a man who cared one whit for what
you might have thought of him. He spat cruel words and mocked
your God and cheered the buzzards dropped to feed on roadkill.
What was all this talk about a new millennium to him?
Weren't the evening and sun the same as always, and nowhere?
Even drunk, he didn't miss, and the cow tumbled down
dead-weight and draining blood, and the good earth shook
on its foundation, knocked off its axis for a visible second,
the good earth clutched at the blood, drug it down, down,
and the neighbor boys hid in the back of their closets.
Here was a stretch of road a man like him could tuck himself
back down and not have to answer to a soul, least of all
some dimwit codger whose cow would stare him straight in the eye.
And then what happened, you'd like to know, as if stories
have endings that conclude or explain, as if stories heal loss,
stop time, weep light, speak truth, change lives, dream souls.
He tumbled himself into his truck, took off toward town
slinging gravel and missing the ditch, his arm out the window
conducting last light on the maples and shagbark hickories,
damning them all to hell, even the burnt stalks of corn
and the useless rail fence and the pigs caked with mud
lost somewhere he was tired of looking, and those bible verses
learned fifty years ago of the good soil and the bad soil,
and it took just a mile before he saw a car coming, and aimed.

# LATE SEPTEMBER

What we're talking about here is the loss
of so many gone away from where we are.

You can say "to heaven," if you believe,
but for the time being they are gone from us,

and we go on sitting in the early mornings,
counting berries weighing down crepe myrtle limbs

or watching the sycamore sense its slightest sway.
Sometimes, late September, I remember them, my dead,

and think that I go out from where I am
as one might go down from a porch

and then take two steps off the bottom board
as if nearing a sound just barely there.

And maybe it matters to have these moments alone
without the ones who mattered most to us,

to have the absence wholly present simply
to stand for a time in the being of not-being.

I'll admit that's hard to comprehend,
especially alone, without another voice

to help along the kind of understanding
that comes when two or more are gathered.

What we're talking about here is the space
between the sounds of the woodpecker's search

for what's beneath the bark, the hunger
each knows and flings against, over and over,

until there's no sound between the lack of sound
and no tree and no field and ever and only the sky.

# WORK STILL TO DO

You should have seen me as a boy, leaping
puddles, my legs above the clouds. Those
were headlines only the grass could read.

There's fieldwork left to do, though—okra
to cut, snap peas to pick—and that place to inhabit
where corn shucks were tossed to the side.

Main Street is all uphill anymore, full of kudzu and talk
of maple leaves that blew the years away. The sermons
were lost, too, when the Prodigal Son took off again.

September feels like resistance, but October is quietly
giving in. The radios told us decades ago
to walk across pastures and not to turn back.

In the night, vandals overturned the headstones others
placed flowers against. I wonder tonight what
the innkeeper will say, a wind so cold, no stable in sight.

# WONDERING ALOUD

So many conversations in the coffee house
revise the chronicles of History, usurp the headlines,
and chart a course toward mercy
                              our country seldom hears.


If you have a soul, some smoldering left inside, maybe
the time has come to bring it words like "and." Its health
may be determined
                    by the poverties it adds unto itself.


So many years now I've rested on clover beds
but never once forgot myself
                              and buried face and arms
to breathe the earth down deep and carry its voice away.


The loveliness of form has brought me back
from who I was, a man itinerant, lulled by memory,
thinking what I've lived
                          has been the only path.


A woman singing of her restlessness makes room for me
to search that self-same road.
                              The moment bears us forth.
We're holding hands against a coming Inquisition.

# HENRY GOWER ROAD

*to Marla Clemments*

This world is another, then another,
yet each time some part remains.
An hour passes, a year, half a life.
Everything once familiar is given back—
as if what we do is become a different person.
Two decades after:  I take the road's
dip down beneath trees overhanging
only then to bear right and soar forth
into open sky—that sense of emerging
into a world made new where no one
is ever lost, where words once shared
hang faint and fragrant on the evening's
still air and my hand out the window
simply reaches and gathers them in.

# A SHORT DISTANCE FROM MOUNTAINS

The voice heard in evening below the others
is rowing itself out over the deepest part
of the lake
      and soon will relinquish the oars.

The fact a mind can meander from moon
to earthworm
      must mean something unforeseen
is possible even when standing in a downpour.

A hummingbird pauses in front of my face,
sails down the length of the porch, then returns.
Does it count
      if one witnesses his own disappearance?

You can't make a coat out of vowels, though you
can imagine how smooth they would feel
or how useless they'd be
      when the air begins to turn.

The truth is
      half a day can pass with nothing more
than the scent of honeysuckle before approaching rain
that never quite finds
      the right place to lay itself down.

# TO A FARMER WHOSE FIELDS ARE RUINED

This last day of the month I see you
standing at a fence; your foot is propped
upon a rail.  In my car I am going
to one of the places I go often—I am
listening to a violin concerto, something
like angels listen to when God's voice
is out strolling again and, alone, they need
to hear their wings.  If I stopped, could we
talk?  Would you put your hand along
my shoulder, or would you point past
the scorched corn stalks, say then
something about men's thoughts, about
the occasion of faith in a heart's demise,
about birds, their nests, the speckled eggs,
the flecks and veins when birth occurs.
I think this day is built of mortar and stillness,
lack of melons.  I've always loved the color
yellow, more bright than squash.  I was
hoping your pensive stare might impress
God himself, that He might grant another
day of creation, allow you anything, whatever
most you've dreamed but never seen, yours
alone.  Not even the birds would know—
not even I would know.  I was hoping this,
though if it happened, how would I know?
I'd have only a feeling, a sense.  I'd look up
to see you shift your weight or turn
in my direction, throw up a hand, a signal,
a sign that says, "It's all familiar.  This world
we ride is holding us in place.  This world has
nests and rails and furrowed brows.  We can
almost hear the wind.  It might be weighted
down, barely able to make the next hill over.
Let's go help it.  Someone tell that hill to move."

# LETTING OUT LINE

Only a little while
      I stood there
in the mist,

looking upstream
      at the willow-oak
leaves loosed

down to float
      the current's
near-rest.

I let drop
      my line and lure,
flicked my wrist

toward a low-limb
      shade of shadows
but missed,

then reeled in
      and tried again,
obsessed

with landing
      a slow motion,
perfectly placed,

unspooling silence
      out of silence
cast,

the kind where briefly
      the moment
is lost,

is pushed
        to an outer edge
straining to resist,

then reappears
        where the bobber
kissed.

# RIDING THE BLOOM DOWNWARD
# THROUGH SHADES OF BLUE

And then there are those days
when nothing seems worthwhile
though I start the morning on cobblestone walkways
under century-old oaks
in the presence of larkspur
and magnolias so thick-limbed
                  I could hide beneath their canopy
and not be found, not even by rain.

Yet the days, the days.
Each a scavenge, a scatter of small seed.
The days a long shiver and wind whipping up.
The days don't know Chagall,
can't find his blue violin,
can't find a person aloft among moons,
can't find an intimate whispering in an ear.

Maybe I'm asking to be surprised,
for the end of the road to say so on and so on.

When the woman stood up from her gardening
to proclaim the holiness of crab apples,
to offer me lemon balm
with its scent surely present
                  on the day of resurrection,

I could only stare at the bumblebee
riding a bloom downward
through shades of blue.

I keep looking for the easel,
the hand and its flourish of brushstrokes.

I keep thinking this thinking
will lead me past thought,
how a jay mazes through an orchard's
lush weight and blossoming
                    to rise up into sky.

The woman bent then to turnip greens,
inspecting their undersides, tugging out weeds,
while I wondered how far
the cantaloupe's runners eventually would reach.

I was already lost in metaphor,
tendril-grope through a rich soil,
when she stood to wipe sweat
                    with the back of her wrist.

How taste the cantaloupe
without breaking it open first?

Or reach for another's hand,
to be guided along,
told of the nuthatch's speckled egg
so easily broken,
                so small in the palm.

# PO-BIZ GHAZAL

Among my friends, few catch the names I drop: Tu Fu, Basho, Li Po.
Dinner parties equal politics, weather. I'd rather wander the mind
    of Li Po.

The only white butterfly for miles around decides to light on my arm!
Ha! Take that! In your macabre face, Edgar Allen Poe!

A train pulls out for Birkenau, straining with the weight of where
it's bound. So many unknown minds still linger in that depot.

Amid the clamoring voices competing and canceling each other out,
let's remember the out-of-tune, mysteriously tuned playing of Harpo.

Whatever wisdom is, and the wholeness it achieves, surely
it has to do with how everything encountered is seen as apropos.

Words are like people—some Ghandi, some Hitler, others
Robin Williams. Sadly, some are Danny DiVito, Cher, Joe Piscopo.

Explanations, too often, are nothing more than strange embellishments.
Listen, you'll forgive me if I don't rehash why I live at the P.O.

Some of the best ideas have backspin on them and veer off
undetected. Even so, I don't trust the ones that storm in all Gestapo.

A cure for this dissident age, its bewilderment and bitterness?
Why not sit and nod agreements with the redbud's wind-nudged tempo?

I wouldn't get too cocky, I tell myself, even if the Pulitzer and Nobel
came along. My own name might turn out to be a simple, overlooked
    typo.

# AS ONE WHO'S BEEN PERMITTED . . .

My crime scenes are traditional
        but with a leaning toward the paradoxical.

Asked to explain, I can think only
        of a cluster of grapes, unripe,
I plucked one at a time
and threw at the head of a neighborhood kid
           I once shushed from my yard,
yelling, "One, the dreams of old men—
two,
        we each hold a radiance . . ."

Like the song said, "I was a lonely teenage
broncin' buck
        with a pink carnation and a pick-up truck,"
none of which I possessed,
though nightly I listened to tree frogs
out my window
        doing their own Sisyphus work in the dark.

Of course, I've wanted happy news.
Of course, I've wanted sidewalks
           strewn with dogwood blooms

and those kinds of fire-lit evenings
flickering on window panes
        where the person playing solitaire
picks up each card and moves it
without reflection
        to the row it's meant to find.

As one who's been permitted
        much bemusement,

a kind of Orpheus in a time of drought,
I nonetheless continue singing,
or humming,
  or tapping a pencil to annoy
the hallowed, unaffected silence.

Here on this wayside heal-all,
   here where the pendulum pulls me apart,
where I sail out these tropes,
I offer revisions, counter-explanations,
versions so complicated
    even I can't translate them,

something reminiscent of the time I held
a magnifying glass
   and a small fire began,
scorching the earth's green name,
widening a black eye
   that follows me still.

All the telltale illusions I said I'd avoid
have come to claim me, it seems;
for I, too,
  spend my days keeping track of dull dreams,
having thought they were grandeur,
   not trendy or cheap.

And now the yard is small, no one to visit—
the boundaries
  are rumors that never reach far
beyond the titmouse worrying a leaf for a nest
most likely some boy
   will be sure to knock down.

# NOT THAT CLEMENCY IS OR IS NOT ON THE WAY

Early morning
        and at the horizon
light brims,

then overspills
        to find this valley
of cedar pantoums

repeating every few yards
        toward the barn
which rhymes

itself in the pond,
        both of them
perfect mimes

keeping to themselves,
        at least for now,
their dreams

of hay and swallows
        and spiders'
elaborate stratagems—

soon the robins and vireos,
        having shaken loose
their names,

will give the whole
        of themselves
in streams and streams

which—please forgive me—
        I've always heard
as hymns.

# HOLDING ON UNDERNEATH THIS SHROUD

I'm on a Funny Campaign, as I like to call it,
    which should prove interesting
since I can't remember jokes that well,
    telling the punch line first
or somewhere in the middle before
    the chicken's halfway across the road.
But I think we'd all agree—something
    needs to happen; it's either soapbox diatribes
or mournful tones and not much in between
    these days. Not to mention how
the literalists are taking over, mistrustful
    of anything that smacks of deeper meaning;
I mean, I saw two of them not even smile
    when two year old Lilly entered the coffee shop,
a miniature statue bearing aloft in each hand
    glorious doughnut holes, raised torches,
one of them already bitten into. Of course
    much of this has to do
with the popularity of anyone while Patty Griffin's
    "Rain" is not our national anthem.
Not that it's funny because it isn't, not even close.
    O how to turn "Where the Streets
Have No Name" into a lullaby, with that much
    leaping toward God—that's the question.
You know you're in trouble when enough people
    go around saying "apropos"
but never stumble onto "enchantment,"
    when too many tether themselves
to mistakes from which they're trying to turn a buck.
    I think of the girl who said, "No,
you need another topic—this one's boring,"
    when the teacher had the class explore
what fascinated them as children. Bored
    by fascination? Are you kidding?
I kept waiting for a punch line. It never came.

# BEFORE THE WHOLE DISPLAY

You can try to squeeze experience
      into certain frames of knowing,
but some days standing next to one person
      opens unforeseen possibilities,
atypical conversations, a memory of larkspur,
and how you came to stand
      in one place instead of another
has no answer beyond second guessings.
      Each person's preoccupations
probably crisscross
      with every other person's,
which makes a workable graph
mostly impossible
      but nonetheless worth imagining.
On one axis the sound of a frog
      a few minutes after midnight
in the deep of a night too proud of its moon,
on another axis
      the swervings of waxwings,
the few hundred that show up one day
to search your lawn,
      and that's just two axes
flashing and flickering among countless galaxies!
Maybe those swervings are too much to grasp
      —multiples multiplying hysterical hunger—
how they remind us how
basically anything teems with so much
unaccounted for,
      never to be traced or kept track of,
even though one can sit before the whole display
not knowing how many droplets fall
      along the swan's glide to readjust its wings
across an otherwise still reflection.

# A PART OF ME HIGH UP

So many people on the street tonight
I begin to wonder
if there isn't some new, happening revolution
   I never got the invite for.

Here I am, though,
holed up in Starbucks,
three women nearby
   plotting schedules
and talking gift cards and letterhead—
and I just want to scream
the word "funeral"
   to see what might occur.

Not to mention (though I will)
two teenagers in espresso stupors,
   heads leaned back against their chairs—
one duded out
in matching black-leather wristbands
and gloves with all the fingers cut off,
chains hanging from every belt loop.

I want to lean in close and whisper,
"Is it Nietzsche?"

"O Little Town of Bethlehem"
takes on something like a four-beat time
with all the headlights
   razing the walls.

Boys on mopeds
   still looking for the Land of Moab—
no goings forth from the old

and none from the everlasting either.

I don't know how to tell anyone,
but as I sit here,
there is a part of me high up,
flapping in the wind—
an insurrection
          no one sees.

No buds in my ears,
no Iphone surfing the web.

What if the whole passing world
is just a glance
          between strangers
so deeply distracted
they're unaware they've even looked up.

And the road now a bypass
around the well at the city gates,
          gone dry anyway,

a new census starting up,
croissants and scones under lights,
          drying out.

# A SEARCH FOR SURVIVORS

Calling out, we don't resemble birds, though like them
we attempt to narrate epiphany, to sing the source
of what our singing signifies.
      We've nothing
of their heft on a branch, swaying slightly up and down,
as though saying itself were somehow barely held aloft
but is.
  And hardly anything wise in what we say
to one another, hardly a moment sufficiently emptied
so that something else, something else, could pour
into its shape.
     Meanwhile, all around, the snow descends,
accumulates, makes the front steps one more hazard
to avoid.  We think ourselves vigilant, discerning, patient
when the world demands our time.  We're practitioners
of the hard season's bearing down, of the town
slowing to stasis.
    A few chimneys release
smoke across the neighborhoods, settling below
the tree line, down among the pansies still holding
their brilliance alongside the rusting swing set
where hornets make their nest.
      From failures calling back to us
we rise each day, add light to dark, shadow to thought, joy
to grief.  Death, of course, keeps a look-out for the slips we make.
We gather what the morning gives, and some of it heals.
We call to those nearby,
      some of whom say our names.

# TRANSPARENCY

I'll slow down
    my life,

not speed it up,
    maybe even become

a new species
    but not one that wants

to conquer anything.
    Rain-showers,

even when stood inside,
    feel like horizons

but intimate,
    like being a hermit

except on the lawn.
    I'll finish Proust

before I take up watching
    flights of swallows.

After that
    I'll start a letter.

*My Country,*
    it will begin,

distilled from the silence
    of morning fog,

to be held up on stems
    of lilacs.

# NO OTHER KIND OF WORLD

Those fog-stalled streets of old movies—
that's the world I want.  And the one, too,
where the old raggedy couple who usually waves

decides, instead, to step inside the café
where I sit drinking coffee, having imagined
I'm an echo fading out across a neighbor's field—

and I find that I have money, enough to buy them
lattes and muffins; and the wife tugs her scarf
from habit, that slow *let-me-get-settled-in-for-*

*the-world-is-so-immense-yet-here-we-are-together*
kind of tug, which happens all too often but
without a word or glance.  And there we sit

surrounded by so many spoons and sugar packets;
and smoke from fires that burn the forests
of the West will never reach us, nor the sounds

of table lamps switched off by widows of this town,
though it is true we can imagine them enough
that when we bow to sip from steaming cups,

we add their lamps and sudden dark to who
we are, since no other kind of world occurs
to us, no other kind of self but one who

doesn't waste the crumbs that soften thumb
and finger, one who tastes a second life,
awake to prayers that course the crowded air.

# OLD MAN PRAYING

Sunday morning, the congregation
thinking of hams and stews and soups,
an afternoon of restful ease, he'd
start a closing prayer we knew
would not be closing soon, naming
the old and sick, the illnesses
our wretched sins had visited
upon us all, the plagues sent down
to show us back to mercy, love,
the healing, holy names of God
we were not worthy to pronounce
or breathe. The children fidgeting
could not deter his pleas for grace
upon *the wicked sinner, Lord,*
the drunk who beat his wife and spent
the rent, the man who cursed him in
the turning lane. He'd heave along,
a coach chastising runts and screw-ups
who couldn't find the net or dribble.
With each fading off, he'd regain
a new path in to hurl petitions
great and small. He'd claim healing
for *Thelma Thompkins' shingles,*
*O Great Physician, and these warts;*
*O keep our hands from all that is*
*unclean, and keep us in thy grace,*
and when we thought he might be done,
he'd find another fervor of fiercer
words trying hard to lift our souls
and say the source of all that can't
be known beyond the tribulations
*and heartaches of your sheep, O God,*
*who cannot find our way to you.*
He'd try to sing the prayer above
the rafters, up to where it broke
and fell apart into phonemes,
vowels, consonants, grunts, the soul
calling out in the wilderness,
aching to know beyond its ache.

# LETTERS

Once he took up residence,
      secluded in that cottage,

he then began the letters
      he claimed he'd always write,

at first one or two a day,
      explaining this stage of life,

his lack of wanting
      what he'd always wanted,

and then more and more pages,
      a month's worth, a year's,

more than he'd written in all his life.
      He thought of little else,

even as he cut and stacked
      the wood he'd need,

preparing for the harshest winter.
      He wrote of what he saw

along his morning walks,
      tadpoles, mossy rocks, pine cones,

enormous upturned roots of fallen trees,
      sometimes a paragraph or more

about the smallest observation
      as if the words had always

been there, ignored for decades
      but now were full of thresholds,

each with countless directions
      from which to amble out.

Not that the letters were always answered.
        Few of them were.

There were so many—who could keep up?
        He did not seem to mind

or notice, and some had moved
        already beyond reportage

into speculation, myth, questions
        with little worry whether

answers, in the end, might matter;
        others were prayer-like, quiet—

like the evening, the trees.
        Mornings brought another thought

to follow, another someone else
        he hadn't written to before.

*Dear old friend*, he'd begin,
        and half the morning

would be given to the flare
        and dim of light along a page,

a kind of warmth
        it was no question anymore

he had to follow.
        Sometimes a cup of tea, a nap,

a pile of leaves to rake and burn,
        a pause to smell the last of autumn

or the first awakenings of dogwood blooms,
        but always then the letters

still to write, the sweetness of endeavor,
       the holiness of pressing all he was

against the blankness of a page.
       Always the day

in all its murmur coming clear.
       Always the motion of his hand

and something else he did not know,
       could not know, would not know

quite the same again.
       And now and then a letter

written to no one in particular
       or someone he'd forgotten,

faceless, some presence from the past;
       and that would be a letter

he would fold and tuck inside a pocket,
       safe with all the others,

some of which,
       after a day of long hours,

he'd unfold carefully,
       smoothing out the creases,

and read to himself,
       happy to hear again

from this almost familiar voice
       he couldn't place exactly,

having come so far
       to say these words to him.

# EACH OF US A MYSTERY WE CANNOT READ ALONE

Assassins, I know you're out there, but what makes you so insistent on
bumping me off? Why waste time tracking my whereabouts, just
    one more
chump poet looking for a fix of rhyme and measure? I've read the sage
Dalai Lama's weigh-in on this matter, and it appears, surprisingly
enough, your efforts will prove unsatisfyingly, eternally
futile, even dimwitted upon further inspection. Try your hand at a
    sonnet,
ghazal, or pantoum, I implore. Occasionally there's applause. Or
    what about
haiku? You've got sabi written all over you. My suggestion: let us
investigate your motives by counting first the syllables you think
justify sliding a bullet in a gun. And look around: we share a
    magnanimous
kingdom with ample room for each of us to do our own wild thing.
    I'll follow
leaves *end-over-ending* this sidewalk, and might I suggest a revision
    to your
mission statement? Maybe add Mozart; long looks out train windows;
needlework. No more looking through scopes, sharpening knives,
obsessing over my half-rhymes and iambic substitutions. I think
    your own
pensées could do wonders for our relationship. We'd be like Ishmael
    and tattooed
Queequeg, wandering around in an Ahab world, each of us a
    mystery we cannot
read alone. Just picture us sitting down to coffee and swapped stories,
soliciting the other's world view. Regarding mine, ever notice how many
times the word *self* is used as a prefix? Not quite as often as
*un-*, which, by the way, means *release from!* I've always thought
    trust the most
vital gift we can offer another, so I guess I'm saying I trust you'll do

what's best in this narrative we've come to share, even if that means

X-ing me out.  After all, I've spent my life arguing for thoughtful,
    precise revision.

You, perhaps better than anyone, know what I mean.  And since
    we're marching to

Zion, the beautiful city of Zion, let's let our joys be known; and
    you, oh you, are mine.

# IN THE PARK

Seven boys seem to think they're birds.
They caw and hoot, running beneath
a stretch of thinned-out trees. They raise
their arms to steer themselves toward each other
and through this maze of limbs dipped low.
Every minute growing louder seems to lessen.
And we talk of a need to witness miracles,
everyone flying so close at each other
until the last possible moment,
                      then veering . . .

# A NEW EARTH

I turn the nation over as if it were
a piece of paper on which someone
has written the word *counterfeit*.
No easy task, lifting that first corner.
Malls, schools, entire neighborhoods
upended, toppled; flat-screens sliding
from walls, cords yanked free, drawers
spilling their tucked-away contents.
Pandemonium, looting, a few trying hard
to gather back things still in reach.  From
where I stand, I count myself fortunate
to see the wide expanse and what has always
been there underneath—

                                a man in a kayak,
for instance, who rights himself and keeps on
paddling, stroke on the left, then on the right.

# PRAYER

Lazing and drunk,
the wasps
     dip to find an angle in to sip again the honeysuckle
(again and again),
        the thick-drenched everywhere scent of it,
bumping against the sugary universe of all that lies before and after.
What's after often alters what's before,
           or makes before
an altar
     and the robin-flits one more movement in the fresh-mown grass,
all of it prayer, even the clouds
          unerring in their slide toward the north
and catalpa blooms shivering down the breeze
           and the studious hawks,
Whitmanic and widening the valley out and farther out.
Well, there's this life to live and the one to follow and a third one
born from the dialogue between.
        Who gets to listen in,
who gets to bury his face in that grammar can't speak it well,
can only stand back stunned and shunned, hungover and drained,
ready to walk the fence row,
        longing to be on another side.
Something human will do if we can't touch divine,
a wrist like a wilted flower, the curve of chin or clavicle,
all of it prayer (again and again),
        child holding a plucked leaf
before her face, beholding its presence beholding her too,
her in its grip, thin-stemmed and sturdy, saying its own prayer,
being what it is
      in the *isness* of its being, being what she holds, *Thou, Thou.*
And where will I not kneel? Nowhere. Nowhere. Even in ash.
And the next moment tamping me down with its verdict
of heron wading—how likely and unlikely—

for time makes its own case,
all of it prayer (again and again), answering and answering,
for the answer hears what the question wants to be,
and the wasp
sates itself in the breeze of the bloom's lip, lip which is prayer,
praying its being,
being its prayer which is answering being.

# I ONCE WAS LOST

I'm writing these long letters,
     as Rilke said I would,

but so far
     I've yet to send them—

unsure just who
     will pull close the lamp

and study the places
     I crossed out the words.

To breathe deeply in
     is a knowing

not easily known.
     Once or twice

it was a field of milkweed,
     another time Walden Pond

pulled from the crease
     of a thumb-worn page.

Sometimes,
     speaking before others,

I know I'm still
     that child

with rolled-up pant legs
     wading upstream

to watch minnows
     dart out ahead

and then stop.
      Like always,

I lose the thread
      of what I'm looking for

as soon as I begin.
      And then—

what else to call it—
      I'm being led

so that anywhere I go
      I'm found.

# Acknowledgments

Grateful acknowledgment is made to the following publications in which poems in this book appeared previously: *Big Muddy, Blue Lyra Review, Connotation Press: an Online Artifact, drafthorse, The Florida Review, The Gettysburg Review, The Hudson Review, IthicaLit, The Louisville Review, The Meadow, New Orleans Review, Ploughshares, Poet Lore, The Southern Review, Southwest Review,* and *Tar River Poetry.*

"Immeasurable," "On the Eve of a New Millennium," and "How Many Lives Do You Have?" appeared in *The Southern Poetry Anthology: Tennessee.* "On the Eve of a New Millennium" appeared in *Hard Lines: Rough South Poetry.*

To friends who make up my wider fellowship, thank you for your generosities: Bill Brown, Tony Earley, Mark Jarman, Lisa Coffman, Bobby Rogers, Jan LaPerle, Clay Matthews, Gary McDowell, Tiana Clark, Marilyn Kallet, Linda Parsons, Andrew McFadyen-Ketchum, Richard Krawiec, Al Maginnes, Chera Hammons, Victoria Clausi, G'anne Harmon, Lola White, Alice Sanford, Margaret Renkl, Darnell Arnoult, Becky Yannayon, Michelle Miller, Kory Wells, and so many others.

Special gratitude to David Till, whose heart-mindedness stands behind me and so many others. I live in a different country because of his influence.

Starla, I can imagine no other world than the one your presence in makes possible. Storie, every day is a beautiful day because you are in it. Eli, we have so many lives to discover.

## About the Author

Jeff Hardin is the author of four previous collections of poetry, including *Fall Sanctuary*, *Notes for a Praise Book*, *Restoring the Narrative*, and *Small Revolution*. His work has been honored with the Nicholas Roerich Prize and the Donald Justice Poetry Prize. A professor of English at Columbia State Community College, he lives in Columbia, Tennessee.

Visit his website at www.jeffhardin.weebly.com.

CPSIA information can be obtained
at www.ICGtesting.com
Printed in the USA
LVOW11s1437260817
546491LV00004B/16/P